Table of contents

Introduction

I f imagination is 'the creative capacity to picture the world otherwise,' we can see how necessary it is to keep us going on the journey of life. Without some imagining of a different future we would, in dark times, succumb to apathy or despair.

Born into a troubled, unpeaceful world (which tried to murder him in his infancy), Jesus grew in wisdom, age and grace, experiencing life with ever more intensity and depth. Gradually, a new imagining of how-things-ought-to-be possessed him. His Father had not created the world for it to be dominated by greed, violence and untruth, but by charity, peace and the truth that sets people free.

The term he used to summarise this new vision was the Kingdom of God, that is, a world under the rule of God's love. Although not capturable in textbook clarity, it was far from being a vague idealism. Jesus spelt it out in action – in healings, forgivings, exorcisings, and in happy gatherings for meals at which all were welcome.

He spelt it out further in his parables – stories of such craft and imagination that they rank among the greatest ever composed.

But the crowning masterpiece of his imagination was the parable-in-action that he created when he performed the first Eucharist at the last supper.

In its original form it is a simple four-part ritual with a few expository words: He took bread, he gave thanks, he broke the bread and gave it to his friends, saying, "This is my Body, given for you." Then the same with the wine: "This is my Blood, poured out for you. Do this in memory of me."

In this spare action he gathered up his whole life, his coming death and resurrection, the future life of his Church, and the final destiny of all things.

Ever since, the Church has been 'doing this' as he said, repeating his simple ritual but spreading it out in time and spelling it out in further words and actions, so that we may the better absorb, and be absorbed by, its richness and mystery. We humans need time and space to properly experience the deepest realities.

In the ceremony of the Mass the original four-part ritual is still there, structuring the whole. We take bread (Offertory), we give thanks (Eucharistic Prayer), we break the bread and share it (Communion). To prepare ourselves for all this, we first read from the scriptures, to alert ourselves to the love of God that is always active in our world but is particularly concentrated for us in our Eucharistic gathering.

Keeping the Bread of Communion in the tabernacle is a reverent prolonging of the Mass, to give us more time for adoration, thanksgiving, and further prayer. The practice of visiting the Blessed Sacrament has been going on in the Church for hundreds of years. It has been the occasion of countless souls coming to God and being drawn into deep union with him. "Like an eternal noontide," wrote the Russian poet Osip Mandlestam, "the Eucharist goes on forever."

Nearly three hundred years ago, St Alphonsus published his book of *Visits to the Blessed Sacrament*, which became, and remains, a classic of devotional writing.

This present book is offered in continuity with the spirit of that lovely work. May it enable its readers to blossom into prayer as they give their time and their hearts to the One who invites them: "Come to me all you who are weary and heavily burdened, and I will refresh you." ■

Richard Tobin, CSsR
St Joseph's, Dundalk, Co Louth

Visit
1
Jesus looked

God pervades our entire being, body and soul, and our entire being, body and soul, responds to God. Prayer is indeed the raising up of mind and heart to God, but we pray, too, with our bodies – with our feet when we walk to Mass or to Holy Communion or on pilgrimage; with our hands when we hold them out to receive the Body of Christ or to make the Sign of the Cross; with our ears when we listen attentively to the Word of God or to uplifting music or to the lovely sounds of God's creation – winds blowing, rain falling, waves breaking, birds singing. We pray, too, with our eyes – when we gaze at the crucifix, or a holy picture, or at the symbols and actions of the Mass.

A man in his middle years only discovered real prayer (as he put it) when the priest in Confession gave him as penance to sit in the church for five minutes and simply look at the tabernacle. "After a first few bewildered and unnerving minutes, I let go of my uneasiness and inclination to flee, and found myself face to face…"

St John Vianney, the Cure d'Ars, noticed a man who spent lengthy periods in the parish church, totally still. The Cure ventured to ask him how he spent the time. The man replied simply: "I look at Him and He looks at me."

Both of these examples recall the Bible's description of prayer as 'seeking the face of God.' 'It is your face, O Lord, that I seek,' says Psalm 27. All methods and practices of prayer are intended to lead to this face-to-face awareness. When it happens, we gently lay aside whatever exercises we have been using: they have done their work.

The Gospels frequently tell of Jesus coming face to face with people and looking at them intently. We do well to notice these occasions and to dwell on the intensity and far-reaching consequences of his gaze.

He looked up at the terrified adulterous woman and asked, "Has no one condemned you?" "No one, sir," she replied. "Well, neither do I," he said. "Off you go now. And don't sin anymore."

He looked at Nathaniel under the fig tree and saw him to be a person without guile.

He looked at Peter on their first meeting and said, "You will be called Cephas… the Rock."

During his trial he looked again at Peter who had just denied him three times. Peter's heart broke, under this gaze of pure love, and 'going out he wept bitterly.' ∎

Prayer

Lord Jesus, here I am in your presence,
Looking *at* you, and looking *for* you,
longing for you to look at me
with your compassionate, understanding eyes.
Do not let me shy away from your gaze.
"I am not here to condemn you," you say to me.
"I died for you. I have given you my body and blood.
Accept my gift and let me see your face, so dear to me.
Yes, I see into your deepest soul,
and know you through and through,
more forgivingly than you know yourself.
As I said to St Angela, 'It was a joy to suffer for you.
And if I had to, I would do it again.'"
Lord Jesus Christ,
have mercy on me, a sinner!

Visit
2
Stillness

All the troubles in the world, said the French philosopher Pascal in the 17th century, come from the fact that we can't sit still in a room, alone.

Nothing in all creation, said Eckhart, the great Dominican theologian in the 14th century, is so like God as stillness.

Earlier yet, God himself said in Psalm 46, 'Be still and you will know that I am God.'

When you become still, beginning with an alert but comfortable physical posture, things begin to happen.

At first there is usually a delicious letting-go – of tension, of uptightness, of having to hold yourself together.

Then, since we're not used to relinquishing control, you may become restless, or agitated, or even a little bit afraid. Smile yourself through this stage. What is there to be afraid of?

Settled again, you'll notice your senses begin to grow sensitive, especially your hearing. Sounds that are there all the time, but that you normally don't notice, begin to become quite distinct – traffic, a distant voice, the little coughs and shuffles of people around you. A world of sounds, and there are you in the centre of it, breathing calmly, beginning to delight in it all.

Your mind may be still jumpy and scattered. Give it something to focus on, a phrase of prayer that repeats itself over and over within you: "God, be merciful to me, a sinner." Or, "Lord, here I am." Or, "Come, Lord, come Lord Jesus." (Or any prayer that is in tune with your soul and your need).

The stillness deepens and gradually suffuses your being, within and without.

Is this stillness like God, as Eckhart said? It's all around you (like God), it's within you (like God), it's ungraspable (like God), it's mysterious (like God), it's healing (like God), it's peace-giving (like God). We could go on.

And will God keep his promise, 'Be still and you will know…'? God always does, in God's good time. ■

Prayer

Lord Jesus Christ, you say to me:
"See, I stand at the door and knock."
So courteous are you, so respectful of my freedom,
so wishful to be in my company.
There are times when I cannot stand myself,
and yet you want to be with me.
How forgiving and how accepting is your love.
It was your custom, the Gospels tell us,
to go off to lonely places to pray,
to be in utter stillness with your Father.
Draw me into that stillness now.
Here in the Blessed Sacrament you are silent and welcoming,
radiating peace and love.
Let your peace wrap me round, and fill every corner of my
being, stilling my racing thoughts and unquiet feelings.
Help me to become still and come to know – that you are
here.
In the stillness may I come to delight in your presence.
You are my Lord and my God forever.

Here I am - *Hineni*

T hroughout the scriptures, whenever God calls someone for a particular task, God usually calls twice, indicating urgency: Abraham! Abraham! Moses! Moses! Samuel! Samuel! And the response of the chosen one is invariably, "Here I am" – *Hineni* in Hebrew.

Much is packed into that simple answer. It signifies total readiness and willingness to be at the Lord's disposal, to do his will at any cost.

This word and attitude is most complete in the response of Mary at the Annunciation: "Look at me! Here I am, the handmaid of the Lord." Scripture also puts the word on the lips of Jesus when it attributes to him the line from Psalm 40, 'Here I am! I come to do your will.'

"My food," Jesus says, "what nourishes my soul, is to do the will of the One who sent me." Down the centuries, countless souls have discovered the same. In doing – or trying to do – the will of God, our humanity reaches its greatest heights.

We grow only gradually into the attitude and truth of "Here I am." It is easy to say, but not easy to mean. We find this if we use it as a word of prayer: "Lord, here I am."

When I begin to say it I am not here at all: I am all over the place, my thoughts and feelings everywhere except here. But I smile at myself and go on quietly repeating, "Lord, here I am," allowing the phrase to gather me into itself and gradually make me present to the Lord.

The first "Here I am" is not very true, but as I repeat it, it becomes more and more true, and I find myself more and more here, more and more attentive to the Lord.

The Lord, on his part, is totally here for me. "Here I am," he says to me. "This is my Body given for you. This is my Blood shed for you." ■

Prayer

My Lord and my God, you know what I am made of.
You know the limitations of my mind and heart.
You know how hard it is for me to collect my scattered
thoughts and give you my full and steady attention.
My mind is like a balloon constantly floating up to the clouds
and having to be brought back again and again from its
wanderings.
And yet, with all my scatteredness – Here I am!
My wish is to be more and more here as the time of my visit
unfolds.
Let the realisation of your presence dawn on me ever more
vividly.
Let the mystery of your everlasting love embrace me.
Let the tenderness of your mercy reassure me.
Let the smile of your delight in me brighten the darkness of
my soul.
I will say over and over the word you have given me to
answer your call:
Lord, here I am!
Lord, here I am!
Forgive whatever is sinful in me.
Heal whatever is unhealthy in me.
Calm whatever is agitated in me.
Soften whatever is hard in me
And fill me with your peace.
Lord, here I am.

Visit
4

A man apart

"**I**n stillness and staying quiet – there lies your strength," says the prophet Isaiah. "Keep peace and you will be safe."

Does sitting still, alone, in a room, have a bearing on the troubles of the world, as Pascal said? The Russian Saint Seraphim of Sarov indicates the answer: "Acquire inner freedom and thousands around you will be liberated." A person with inner peace and freedom is a calming, reassuring presence wherever they go.

Jesus was such a person. Why did people flock to him in such numbers? Because he healed and delivered them from evil? Yes. Because he spoke, with authority, words that broke open their hearts? Yes. But his words and actions flowed from the man he was. By all accounts he was a person who was profoundly at one with himself, contagiously free and at peace in the depths of his being. Such a person will attract people even if he never healed or spoke with burning words.

Jesus's inner strength was constantly nourished by his prayer. Again and again in the Gospels we hear of him going off to a lonely place to pray. For example, in the first chapter of St Mark we read that after a long, busy day and a few hours sleep in a crowded house, he slipped out, long before dawn, and went to a desert place to pray. In imagination we can follow him and watch a while, but only at a distance – who would dare to intrude on that profound communion between Jesus and his

Father? We can only stand in awe in the presence of such intense prayer, Father and Son bonded together by the Spirit of Love flowing between them.

And yet we are drawn to this mystery, and, indeed, invited into it! "If anyone loves me, my Father will love them, and we will come to them." Again and again Jesus talks of us being gathered into the love between himself and the Father, into the circle of love that we call the Blessed Trinity.

Philosophers and theologians speak of this mystery as at once fascinating and fearful. We are drawn to it and at the same time shrink from it in awe. Humankind cannot bear very much of such intense reality. But, with God's help, we learn. "We are put into this world a while," says the poet Blake, "to learn to bear the beams of love." ■

Prayer

Lord Jesus, I underestimate you so seriously.

I think of you too sentimentally, too piously,

missing the strength and power of your personality.

It was no harmless weakling that electrified the crowds in

Galilee and awoke the murderous fury of the powers in

Jerusalem.

It was no wilting lily that sweated blood in Gethsemane

and shed that blood on Calvary.

All this memory of you is gathered here in the Eucharist.

Help me to immerse myself in it more and more,

so that I may come to know you more truly

and be fascinated by you all over again.

In the Blessed Sacrament you hide yourself for my sake,

so that the beams of your love and glory will not overwhelm me.

I bless you for such courtesy and consideration.

It leads me to dare to come into your presence,

to enter into your stillness,

to ask you to draw me into your communion with the Father.

Lord, here I am. Let it be done to me according to your word.

Visit
5

"**H**umankind," says the poet TS Eliot, "cannot bear very much reality." Reality is so dense, so various, so mysterious, that it can overwhelm our poor, limited minds.

Looking up at the heavens on a starry night can fill us with wonder, but it can also make us afraid. "The silence of the infinite spaces between the stars makes me tremble in awe," said the French philosopher Pascal.

Likewise a great joy or grief or longing can be too much for us.

So God, who knows our limitations, gives us the gift of time. God spreads reality out for us across hours and days and years, so that we may absorb it little by little, and not be overwhelmed by having to meet it all at once.

God himself is Ultimate Reality. If God were to show himself to us now face to face, the experience would shatter us. Mercifully, God filters his presence to us through all God has created and within the events and encounters of daily life.

Over countless centuries God gradually educates his beloved humanity to sense and find him within the world of time and space. Patiently God brings his chosen people to their point of greatest sensitivity in a young girl from Nazareth. Time reaches its most intense moment and, at Mary's 'Yes,' the Son of God is born into our world. Time and eternity have intersected. Or rather, time is now contained in eternity. ■

Prayer

My Lord and my God,
in the Holy Eucharist you hide your glory
in the humble forms of bread and wine,
so that the full reality of your presence will not overwhelm us.
I thank you for this considerate mercy.
And yet, although you are hidden, you are wholly and
personally present, giving yourself to us in total love.
I thank you for bringing me into your presence.
I thank you for the hunger, the hope, the longing that
prompted me to come to you.
I thank you for the measureless ages of time that have
brought us, you and me, to this moment.
In return I can only offer you my limited time – time to rest in
your company and allow your loving presence to surround me
and quieten my agitations and anxieties.
I bring to you so many hurts that need healing,
so many failures that need forgiving,
so many prayers that need answering,
that I hardly know where to begin.
But you will meet me with your usual patience
and draw out my deepest prayers from my confusions.
Lord Jesus Christ, have mercy on me, a sinner.

Visit
6
Holy Spirit

"**I** believe that every time Mass is celebrated the Holy Spirit is poured out on the world." This quiet declaration of faith was made by the poet Padraig Colum in a Manhattan restaurant while talking with two friends. It's the confident statement, not of a theologian, but of a man with an insight born of lifelong immersion in the Eucharist.

A Redemptorist priest, now gone to his reward, cherished the remark of a poor widow who had lost her husband when her five children were still small and social welfare was unknown. "They are a credit to you," he said to her one morning outside the church. "'Twas the Mass that reared them," she replied simply, referring to the fact that every morning, no matter how bad things were, she began each day with an early Mass. It gave her the courage and capacity for sacrifice she needed to face her daily struggle. An outpouring of the Holy Spirit, no doubt – the life and energy of God flowing into her.

Mass could not happen without the Holy Spirit. With his last breath on the cross Jesus breathed the Spirit on the world – the word 'spirit' meaning 'breath.' The same Breath of God blows gently but powerfully over us at Mass.

It is by the Holy Spirit flowing into them that the bread and wine become the body and blood of Christ. We pray for this beforehand. The priest spreads his hands above the gifts and says, "Let your Spirit come upon these gifts to make them holy, so that they may become for us the Body and Blood of our Lord

Jesus Christ." Then it's as if the bread and wine say humbly, "*Hineni!* Here we are! Let it be done to us according to your Word," and they are transformed. If only we were as humble and compliant!

We do pray, though: "May we who are nourished by his body and blood be filled with his Holy Spirit…"

The poet Elizabeth Spires writes about her Sunday morning Mass:

> *There on the bare table*
>
> *The plate of bread, the cup.*
>
> *I have come to sit quietly*
>
> *To be filled up.* ∎

Prayer

Lord of my life,

when you walked our roads

and encountered people who were lost and struggling,

your aliveness and vivacity enchanted them.

Your vitality was contagious and invigorating.

The Holy Spirit, the Lord and giver of life,

had filled your being from your very conception.

Risen from the dead, your first gift to us was the Holy Spirit.

"Receive the Holy Spirit," you said to your disciples,

and you breathed on them,

sighing into them the Holy Breath of Life.

From the Eucharist your Spirit continues to give life to the world.

I have come here to be refreshed by your Spirit,

to have all that is dead in me revived,

all that is withered in me made green again,

all that is sinful in me washed away.

I have come to sit quietly

to be filled up.

Behold the man

"**B**ehold the man," said Pilate, presenting the half-destroyed Jesus to the crowd.

Ironically, those words sum up all that we Christians have to say to the world.

If you want to know what life is really about, Behold the man.

If you want to know what humanity is like at its best, Behold the man.

If you want to know what humanity is like at its worst, as we destroy each other, Behold the man.

If you want to know what sin is like, Behold the man.

Above all, if you want to know what God is like, Behold the Man.

This is the most revealing thing God has ever told us about himself, the most powerful statement God has ever made to the world.

"Nature can lead us to God," said the French poet Paul Claudel, "but not to a crucified God." Were we here till doomsday we would never of our own accord have tumbled to the fact that God loved the world this much.

When, through over-tiredness, your small child gets into a tantrum and spits fire and fury at the world, you gather him into your arms and hold him tight, absorbing his cries and blows, overcoming his violence with your love, and gradually lulling him into peace. This is an act of redemption.

The two arms of the cross are the two arms of God around the world, holding God's children tight while they vent their fury upon God's Son. Though you do your worst, God says to us, I will go on loving you with an everlasting love.

"The eternal God is your dwelling place," said Moses, reassuring his people, "and underneath everything are the everlasting arms."

"Surely he has borne our griefs and carried our sorrows," the Church reminds us in the words of the prophet Isaiah.

Jesus said to St Angela of Foligno as she meditated on his Passion, "It was no joke loving you so much. But it was a joy for me to suffer for you, and if I had to, I would do it again." ■

Prayer

My Lord and my God,

in the Eucharist we recall your Passion and Death:

"This is my body given for you, my blood shed for you."

How can I ever thank you enough for being the Lamb of God,

who takes away the sins of the world!

On the cross you absorbed into yourself

all our anger and violence, our lust and greed, our envy and bitterness.

Forgive the sins of mine that filled your cup of sorrows.

Burn into my mind the memory of your Cross and Passion.

so that I will never forget you,

never take you lightly again,

never underestimate the seriousness and power of your love.

I place myself at the foot of your cross and pray,

as so many Irish people have prayed down the years,

"O King of the Friday …

let some fruit from the Tree of your Passion

fall on us this night."

Visit
8

Where are you?

In the Gospels Jesus asks many questions, all of them searching and worth pondering: Who are you looking for? What do you want me to do for you? Who do you say that I am?

But God's questions began in the Garden of Eden. Walking in the garden in the cool of the evening, God called to the man and the woman, "Where are you?" They were hiding in the bushes, ashamed after their disobedience, their vain attempt to be gods themselves, afraid to show their faces.

All of us are shy about showing our faces. Some primordial sense of unworthiness, or even worthlessness, makes us shrink from revealing ourselves, even to those who love us most. There is some degree of pretence and untruth in all our relationships. We can cry out to God in the words of the psalm, "Lord, show me your face!" Yet we hesitate to show our own. When God calls to us, "Where are you?", we hide.

In what bushes? All the preoccupations and busy-nesses of life – work, play, possessions, making money, chasing rainbows. We can even hide from God in our prayers when we are more concerned with performing them than allowing them to bring us face to face with God, which is what they are for.

Patiently, God goes on calling, "Where are you? Let me see your face, shame and all. Trust me. I made you. I know you through and through. No need to be afraid. I only want you to be all you have it in you to be."

We have two mysteries to contend with here: the mystery of God whom we know so imperfectly, and the mystery of our 'self', also poorly known. As the old song says, 'There's a depth in my soul never sounded nor known.' Who is this I, this *me*, this *self* around which my whole life revolves? Ultimately we can only sigh and smile, and learn to live with our own elusiveness and mystery. And, by the same token, with the elusiveness and mystery of everyone else. Our mysteriousness somehow mirrors the mysteriousness of the One who made us in his image and likeness.

Learning to live with mystery, being amazed by it, delighting in it, is part of our growing to maturity as human beings. At its heart, we know, is the most astonishing mystery of all – the great God who made us and calls longingly to us: "Where are you?" ■

Prayer

Jesus, you are the image of the invisible God,
as St Paul tells us.
Because of you, the Way, the Door,
I can approach the Father,
can even dare to call God Father.
Because of you and your assurance of the
Father's merciful love,
I can emerge from my hiding places,
knowing that even my worst sins and
blunders are forgiveable,
and that the Father runs to meet me like the
Prodigal Father in your story,
welcoming me home and spreading a feast for me,
the feast of the Eucharist.
Lord, here I am!
Hungry for truth, love, mercy, and the Bread of Life.
Only say the word and my soul shall be healed.

Visit
9   Where is your brother?

The story of Cain and Abel, in chapter four of Genesis, seeks, like the Adam and Eve story, to give expression to the flawed character of human nature. This time the focus is on our propensity for violence and killing.

After Cain has murdered his brother, God asks his second searching question, "Where is your brother?" That question is meant to disturb us all.

Like Cain, we instinctively tend to shrug off responsibility – "Am I my brother's or sister's keeper?" - but, of course, we are. Both Old and New Testaments leave us in no doubt. 'Love the Lord your God and love your neighbour as your other self' are the two greatest commandments.

Once we say 'yes' to his invitation to follow him, we begin the difficult task of learning to love others as Jesus loved them. We can never complacently pursue our own spiritual life and forget the neighbour. God's question constantly disturbs us: "Where is your brother?"

Without our realising it, the Eucharist educates us to love our neighbour. Those astounding words, "This is my blood poured out for you and for all," work their way into our consciousness, and our Lord's high ideal of love takes root in us. His total giving of himself, repeated in Mass after Mass, becomes for us the ultimate measure of love. Unknownst to us, it constantly judges our own poor quality of loving and summons us to do better.

"This is my body given for you" is the standard of love to which we are called. It is clearly and beautifully true for married couples and parents. But every giving of time, attention and help to others, however modest, is a reaching towards the noble ideal of our Lord.

Again without our realising it, Mass is all the time broadening our minds and expanding our capacity for concern. Praying together for 'the Church throughout the world,' for pope and clergy and all God's people (including the dead), quietly opens in us a largeness of vision that takes us beyond our merely personal preoccupations.

The simplest Christian people, nourished by weekly or daily Mass, develop a truly 'catholic' sensibility – that is, 'all-embracing' or 'in tune with the whole of reality.'

More than it ever knows, the world is upheld by such noble souls. ■

Prayer

Lord Jesus, you tell me

"Love the Lord your God with all your heart and mind and
soul and strength, and love your neighbour as your other self."

How poorly I have responded to these two commandments.

How complacently I have assured myself

that I do no great harm to anybody and mind my own
business.

You remind me that my neighbour's need is my business,

that I am my brother's and my sister's keeper.

Show me how I may come to the aid of others,

not in a nosey and intrusive way,

but quietly, respectfully and generously.

Expand my mind and heart and prayers

to be hospitable to the needs and sufferings of the whole
world.

Help me to see things as you, with a breaking heart,

saw them from the cross.

I adore you, O Christ, and bless you,

Because by your holy cross you have redeemed the world.

Joy

The Roman poet Virgil wrote of 'the tears at the heart of things.' Samuel Johnson, the English writer, said that "life is more to be endured than enjoyed" – himself being no stranger to ill-health, depression and religious anguish. In our prayer, 'Hail Holy Queen,' we 'send up our sighs' from 'this valley of tears.'

Who could quarrel with these descriptions of human life? For all our progress and sophistication the last hundred years have been the most violent and murderous in human history, causing more tears to flow than ever before.

Can anyone, with open eyes, speak of joy in such a world? "Humankind," said Eliot, "cannot bear very much reality." Must we shut out most of reality in order to have any peace or joy at all?

Yet Jesus spoke of wanting his joy to be in us and of our joy being full.

Scholars mention 'the catholic *and*' or 'the catholic *both-and.*' Much as we might like to simplify life into 'either-or' terms, we must learn to live with its contradictions. We are *both* body *and* soul; Jesus was *both* God *and* man; God is *both* beyond us *and* close to us; life is *both* sad *and* joyous, even at the same time. Our Christian intuition is that Jesus experienced deep joy even as he suffered on the cross. We cannot dismiss such apparent contradictions: too many saintly people have testified to similar experiences. Tears of sorrow and tears of joy often flow from the same source.

Our strong tradition is that gloom is not a healthy state to settle into. Perhaps too many of us cling to our sadness and cynicism, taking gloomy pleasure in a listless despondency, neglecting to hope for the joy God intends for us.

"Ask and you shall receive," said Jesus. So we ask for light and joy to flow into our souls, to lift up our hearts, to give a lightness to our step, a song to our hearts, a pleasantness and peacefulness to our presence with our friends.

With God's help it is possible to be surprised by joy. ■

Prayer

Lord Jesus Christ, true God and true man,
it is clear from the Gospels
that you were a man who knew intense joy,
in spite of your sensitivity to the pain of the world.
The pressure of joy in your soul often made you cry out.
You cried out from the intensity of love for your Father.
You cried out from your passionate love for humanity.
You cried out from joy in creation.
You took delight in the flight of birds,
in the flowers blowing in the field,
in the sheep following the shepherd,
in the fishermen hauling in their nets,
in the woman baking her bread.
Too often I am dull and unresponsive to all such things,
too wrapped up in myself,
too much in love with my own sadness.
Call me out of myself, into laughter and playfulness,
into delight in life and its mysteries,
into joy in you, risen from the dead
and wanting my resurrection too.
Surprise me with joy!

Visit
11
God speaks

People have always been aware of powers beyond the ordinary at work in the world.

They called them gods. They offered them prayers and sacrifices, but their predominant attitude to them was fear and anxiety. These gods were capricious and unreliable; it was hard work keeping in with them, and you never knew how many of them there were or which of them was the most powerful. To be on the safe side, you made an altar and offerings 'To an Unknown God,' as St Paul found them doing in Athens, in case there was one more that they ought to placate. Yet these gods were, in various ways, inklings of the true God who would eventually make himself known.

The Old Testament can be read as the record of God's gradual making known of himself to the chosen people, weaning them from false gods – or non-gods – and patiently educating them about his nature and ways. It took God hundreds of years: we humans are not easy to teach!

The key realization in the Old Testament is that God is a God who speaks, in a personal way, to human beings. Again and again we encounter the phrase 'God says' or 'It is the Lord who speaks,' as God unveils (which is the meaning of the word 'reveals') his mind and heart and nature to humanity.

Eventually, 'in the fullness of time,' humanity is ready, in the person of a young woman named Mary, to receive God's final, definitive word about himself. This time it is not a limited spoken word, but the Word made flesh. Mary says, "Here I am," and God's expression of himself becomes a living human being in her womb. From now on, Jesus is the defining word of God in the light of which all other words of God make sense. All the centuries of God speaking were leading up to this.

If you want to know God and what God is really like, Behold the man! ■

Prayer

My Lord and my God, Word of God made flesh,
what a fullness of meaning and mystery we have in you!
In you the great invisible God of power and might,
who made the universe and sustains it in being,
has unveiled himself in human form.
When you in turn promised yourself to us in the Eucharist as
our food and drink, many turned away from you in disbelief.
"Will you also go away?" you asked Peter.
And he replied, "Lord, who would we go to? You alone have
the words of eternal life."
If you asked me now "Will you also go away?"
I would have to make the same reply.
Who else is there who can make sense of everything?
Who else could be the light of the world?
I bless and thank you, Lord, for being there –
for being in my life, in my mind and heart,
a steady brightness in an uncertain world, a shining delight
when I allow the thought of you to fill my being.
Come, Lord! Come, Lord Jesus! Let me see you afresh.
Let your nourishing love flow into me,
bringing to life all that has wilted and died in me.
Send me out into the world with your peace in my soul
and the radiance of your presence about my person.

Visit
12   Wrestling with God

Our need in prayer is not to escape into a pious, unreal world, but to be met where we are, in the total reality of our being, body and soul, warts and all. It's little good unless the entirety of our humanity is gathered into the presence of God. This means bringing our angers, our resentments, our sexual and emotional confusions, our sins before God – for healing, for forgiveness, for sorting out and eventual transformation.

"I spent the first fourteen years in the desert," said one of the early Christian hermits, "praying to be delivered from anger."

Any of the human passions can get a grip on us like that. Patient, persistent prayer, time spent in total honesty with God, is necessary for our being set free. Such prayer will often be more of a struggle than a pleasant conversation.

In the Book of Genesis the name Israel is given to Jacob after he has wrestled all night with an angel. Israel, the angel tells him, means 'the one who wrestled, or struggled, with God.' It's a name that fits us all.

"For years I wrestled with the devil," an old monk told the Greek author Kazanzakis, "until he finally gave up and left me. Now I wrestle with God."

"And hope to win?" asked the writer.

"No. And hope to lose," answered the monk.

Our struggle with God often revolves around our sexual longings and affections. Even the best of people can find themselves in turmoil of this kind. The strength of our desires can at times be overwhelming and turn a previously serene life into panic and distress. All this belongs in our prayer. It probably won't be serene prayer; more likely it will be anguished and disorderly. Sometimes more like an inner howl of near-despair. Most people know the truth of St Augustine's cry, "Lord, make me chaste, but not yet!"

Much struggle, and sometimes failure, has to be gone through as we mature into sexual peace.

'Sexual peace' is a good term to keep in mind, whatever our walk in life. It's an ideal to long for, a state to pray for. It can be a steadying thought, helping us keep things in perspective in our overheated culture. ▪

Prayer

Lord Jesus, here I am, in all my humanity.

You know me through and through.

You know what it is to be tempted in every way,

and to be anguished in your temptations

as you were in the Garden of Gethsemane.

You were like us in all things except sin.

I bless you, Lord, for taking our human nature

and showing us how precious it is to God.

I bless you for the understanding you show in the Gospels

for those whose loving sometimes goes astray.

"I will not condemn you," you said to the woman they

wanted to stone.

"Off you go, but sin no more. You are too good for things like

that."

Lord, be likewise merciful to me, a sinner.

Grant me peace.

Visit
13   You are my God

The first rule of prayer, says that fine spiritual guide Dom John Chapman, OSB, is "pray as you can, and not as you can't." It's a liberating rule that can save us from much futile straining. But it does not mean that we should confine ourselves to the small prayer repertoire we are used to and not try to broaden our capacities.

The liturgy, the public prayer of the Church, rescues us from the limitness of our own language and imagination by gathering us into larger and more various ideas and experiences.

The Church has made her own the hundred and fifty psalms in the Bible, prayers composed and used by generations of people seeking God's face. There are psalms for all seasons and situations – praise, thanksgiving, complaint, desolation, lament, even some for giving out to God!

Many phrases from the psalms have become familiar through their use in the liturgy: 'The Lord is my shepherd, there is nothing I shall want'; 'The Lord is compassion and love'; 'Have mercy on me, God, in your kindness'; 'Like the deer that yearns for running streams, so my soul is yearning for you, my God.'

Any of these phrases can be murmured over and over and allowed to gradually expand our minds and enlarge our prayer. But it is worthwhile reading entire psalms regularly to be drawn into the rich experience they give words to, and into the mind of Christ who prayed them constantly, having learnt them at his mother's knee. A piercing moment for her on Calvary would have been to hear him saying, before his final sleep, the psalm she said with him at bedtime when he was a boy: "Into your hands, O Lord, I commend my spirit."

Perhaps the central statement of the psalms is 'You are my God,' which occurs many times and is implicit throughout. These four short words, unremarkable at first glance, carry a power and intensity that can shake the soul.

They are, of course, a complete declaration of faith. Said attentively, and repeated slowly, they bring us face to face with the awesome mystery of God. Oftentimes you won't get beyond the first word, 'You.' To know and address God as 'You' is a joy that needs no further words. ■

Prayer

You are my God, Lord Jesus Christ.

My God and my all.

You – You – You –

You are my God.

What a gift, to know you personally, to be able to say You.

You are no vague spiritual force,

but a personal companion with whom I can converse,

to whom I can confide my innermost thoughts and secrets,

to whom I can trust my entire life.

Here, in Bread and Wine, you entrust yourself to me.

You speak personally to me as my friend and companion.

I, who so often feel worthless, am desired by You.

You, through whom all things were made, enjoy my

company.

You, the image of the Invisible God, call me 'friend'!

I bless you, Lord, and thank you.

You are my God!

Visit
14

Desire

The first chapter of St Mark's Gospel contains an account of a full and busy day in the life of Jesus. It is a Sabbath and he spends a long time in the synagogue, a devout Jew among other devout Jews on whom his teaching makes a deep impression.

In a dramatic incident he frees a tormented man from an unclean spirit. The people are astonished.

Towards evening he goes to the home of the brothers, Simon and Andrew. There he cures Simon's mother-in-law of her fever. As the word spreads they begin to bring him the sick and the troubled so that 'the whole town came crowding round the door.'

Eventually all disperse to their homes and the house settles down to sleep.

In the morning, long before dawn, Jesus slips out quietly and goes to a lonely place to pray.

The depth of that prayer is beyond our imagining: the world had never before known such intensity. It still goes on, of course – that profound communion of Father and Son in the Holy Spirit. Here in the church we can become aware of it as truly as if we had been watching in that lonely place. Indeed, we are drawn into it, into that circle of love which is the Blessed Trinity.

Later, Simon and the others arrive and speak a sentence which, in its fuller meaning, describes the whole human condition: "Everyone is looking for you." That is the quest that underlies all the frantic efforts of human life. That is the 'something more' that agitates all our restlessness, though we may not yet realise it. The desires and hopes that keep us alive seem to be merely for other things – wealth, pleasure, status. But the deepest desire of the soul is for the one who is 'the Way, the Truth and the Life.' The English writer G.K. Chesterton goes so far as to say that the man who knocks on the door of the prostitute is really looking for God! The desire under the desire.

St Augustine's famous sentence is always worth remembering:

"You have made us for yourself, O God, and our hearts are restless until they rest in you." ∎

Prayer

Everyone is looking for you, Lord, including me.

That is why I have come, yet again, to your house.

Your door is always open, your welcome warm and joyful,

your table set with Bread and Wine.

A greater wonder than our searching for you

is your continual searching for us,

the Good Shepherd seeking his lost sheep.

There are times, Lord, when I'm lost as lost can be,

times when my immediate desires obscure my deepest

desire of all and divert me from your way.

Over and over again I have to re-find my bearings

and rediscover you.

So, here I am –

come again to be in your presence,

come again to be healed and forgiven,

come again to be nourished by your love,

come again to be filled with your peace.

I hardly dare to say "I love you,"

but I can dare to say "I desire to love you."

And that, St Augustine assures us, is enough.

Visit
15
Who am I?

The name Tiffany might seem to connote all that is modern and secular. In fact, it is a variant of the Greek word *theophany*, which means a manifestation of God, such as those given to Moses, narrated in the Book of Exodus.

The word 'epiphany' has much the same meaning – a showing forth, a revelation. The Church applies it particularly to the event of the Wise Men fom the East, celebrated on January 6th. But other epiphanies are celebrated on the Sundays following – the Baptism of Jesus in the Jordan, the marriage at Cana. These, too, were revelations of the divine reality of Jesus, the shining out of his godliness. But, of course, in the light of the Resurrection, every incident in the Gospels has the quality of an epiphany. When we read thoughtfully, even a single sentence can shine out for us with the divine presence.

Picture the scene by the Jordan river: John preaching urgently about the coming judgement of God and leading people into the water to be ritually washed, as an act of preparation. Jesus, too, comes to be immersed, identifying himself totally with his people. But a deeper identification occurs.

As he emerges from the water, the heavens open above him – are 'torn open,' St Mark says, as if a force from beyond this world is urgently breaking in. The voice of the Father is heard: "You are my Beloved Son. My soul delights in you." And the Spirit, like a dove, descends on him.

A theophany, indeed: the Holy Trinity being manifested to the world, the identity of Jesus being revealed and his mission inaugurated.

All that happened to Jesus by the Jordan happens to us in our baptism. Our truest identity is revealed – "You are my beloved child" – the Spirit is given to us, and we are set on a way of walking through this world in the footsteps of our elder brother, Jesus, charged with his mission of embodying the Kingdom of God.

Who am I? At turning points in life – death of parents, loss of job, the approach of our death – the question can trouble us. Our names situate us among our people, our work gives us only a temporary sense of belonging, our death seems to evaporate everything.

But our deepest identity remains forever. Who am I? "You are my beloved child," God tells us, "and my soul delights in you." ■

Prayer

Lord Jesus Christ, Friend and Brother,

here in your presence I am also in the presence of the Father

and the Holy Spirit,

since all three are one and inseparable.

Your Eucharist is a celebration of the Trinity

and holy communion an entering into your circle of love.

I am staggered by the richness of this mystery;

my poor mind cannot take it in.

I am constantly in need of your epiphanies,

to awaken my soul to divine realities.

I am also in need of continual reassurance

that, far from being a hopeless nonentity,

I am precious in your eyes, dear to your heart.

Draw me into ever deeper realisation

that day after day heaven is open above me,

that your Holy Spirit flows into me with love and forgiveness,

that the Father is always saying to me, as he said to you:

"You are my beloved child; my soul delights in you."

Visit
16 Hope springs eternal

More than we usually realise, we live by hope.

Particular hopes may evaporate, but an underlying general hope continues to sustain us. It's a sense that, somehow, a promise has been made to us and that, somehow, it will be kept. Even without a specifically religious faith, such hope remains in the human heart.

Gitta Sereni wrote several books exploring the mystery of evil in human life. One was a biography of Albert Speer, the Nazi who had managed to survive the Nuremberg trials and many years in prison. He was tormented by awareness of his complicity in the Nazi atrocities against the Jews, craving forgiveness and redemption yet unable or unwilling to admit his guilt.

Discussing this with Sereni, an interviewer said naively, "I suppose we all have to come to some forgiveness of these crimes?" Sereni was appalled. "Oh no," she said. "Such forgiveness is beyond the capacity of human beings. Only a God could forgive such evil. I don't believe in God," she went on, "but I hope there is a God who can cope with such horror."

A profound intuition, this, of the human need for God, for someone who can encompass everything, even undiluted evil. "I don't believe... but I hope..."

Deep in our souls we really long for judgement – for a final and complete rendering of justice and truth concerning the whole human enterprise. We shrink from it, of course, all too conscious of our personal guilt. And yet we hope that, somehow, ultimately, 'all shall be well,' as Julian of Norwich put it, 'and all manner of thing shall be well.'

We can anticipate the final judgement, even now, by availing of another lovely gift of God, the Sacrament of Reconciliation or Confession. In that rich encounter with unbounded love, we can face and name the worst about ourselves and know that it will not destroy us. Rather, we hear again the splendid, forgiving, liberating words of Jesus to the adulterous woman:

"Neither will I condemn you. Go in peace, and do not sin anymore." And we are embraced and made whole and human again in the everlasting arms of the Prodigal Father.

No psychiatrist, no guru, can do that for us. ∎

Prayer

Jesus, my Lord and my God,

why should I fear judgement, either in Confession or after my death, when it is you who are my judge?

Not an impartial judge either, but one biased irrevocably in my favour, a judge who died to take away my sins and the sins of the world.

I recall the words of St Francis de Sales: "I would rather be judged by God than by my own mother."

Yes, Lord, sin is ugly and destructive.

I squirm at the thought of my own wrongdoings.

At times a deep sense of shame and remorse comes over me.

I feel, painfully, the truth of our words before Holy Communion:

"Lord, I am not worthy to receive you…"

But I come to you, not because I am worthy

but because I need you, and you invite me:

"Come to me, all you who are weary and heavily burdened."

"Take and eat; this is my Body, given for you, my Blood shed for you."

Visit
17   Adoration

'**I** kiss my hand to the stars,' begins a stanza by Gerard Manley Hopkins, perhaps echoing what is thought to be the origin of the word 'adore' – kissing one's hand towards a god one wanted to honour.

In the Bible the gesture of adoration was usually to fall down, or to prostrate oneself, before God.

Whatever gesture or posture we use, adoration is essentially directing our whole being towards God. When words accompany it, they will be words of praise and thankgiving, joyously poured out. But sometimes we will be so full of reverence and love for God that no words can express it. Then some bodily gesture comes naturally.

Our lives could be described as the longing and the search for someone to adore.

It's what we are born for – to cast ourselves down in joyful, total homage to the someone to whom we know we owe our entire being.

It's an exhilarating thing to do, and necessary for our well-being. When, through ignorance or inhibition or self-preoccupation, we cannot bring ourselves to do it, our humanity remains in some measure unfree, even stunted, and our joy remains sadly confined.

Even to say deliberately and honestly to another human being, "I adore you," makes the heart leap in pure delight. A pent-up force is released in us and we are taken out of ourselves.

When the beauty and greatness of God stirs us and a surge of adoration wells up in us, we can know a joy and release that is beyond all others: This is what I was born for!

From the beginning adoration was one of the four 'ends of the Mass,' the others being thanksgiving, asking for grace, and making atonement for sin. These are the four principal instinctive responses of the soul to God.

A keen deprivation that goes with unbelief is having no one to thank, no one to adore, no one to cry out to for grace and forgiveness. The spontaneous instincts remain, though, and the unbelieving world resorts to the limp, impersonal 'thankfully' and 'hopefully' to replace the vigorous 'thank God' and 'please God' that were the genuine prayers of more Christian times. The other two instincts, to ask and to repent, remain unreplaced, so the heart's cries for grace and mercy are stifled and unexpressed.

What a desolate place the universe would be if there were no face for us to seek, no eyes to gaze upon us with love, no You for us to talk to, no everlasting arms to uphold us all, no transcendant God to adore! ■

Prayer

Lord Jesus Christ,

my prayer and my life are so timid and bland.

Free me from my half-heartedness and inhibition.

Release my capacity for exuberant praise and adoration,

for forgetting myself in the very thought of You.

Let me say the 'Glory to God' at Mass with a new, deliberate

wholeheartedness.

Let me say 'Thanks be to God' more often and more

consciously.

Let me discover the joy and expansiveness

of adoring you all the time,

and especially here in the Eucharist.

I kiss my hand to you, Lord, in love and reverence.

I join my praise and adoration to that of all creation.

It is so right to give you thanks and praise!

I bow down before you, my Lord and my God.

Visit
18

Intercession

"**P**ray for my soul," says the dying King Arthur in Tennyson's poem. "More things are wrought by prayer that this world dreams of."

A persistent human intuition is that not only are things 'wrought by prayer' but somehow the world is sustained in being by the presence and prayers of devout, hidden souls. In the Bible, this intuition is expressed in the constant intercession (from the Latin *go between*) of Moses for his grumbling, rebellious people. It is vividly embodied in the story of Abraham interceding on behalf of Sodom and Gomorrah in chapter 18 of Genesis. "Will you spare the city if there are fifty good people there?" "Very well," says God, "I will spare the city." "Forty-five?" Abraham continues. "Forty? Thirty? Twenty? Ten?" "For the sake of ten," God says, "I will not destroy it."

At every moment of every day intercession rises before the face of God from every corner of the world. Why? Because people love one another and love God, and intercession brings these two loves together.

When you intercede for someone you hold them and the Lord in your thought and affection so that they mingle, the person carried by your concern into the heart of God, and God's love channelled through you into the heart of the one you pray for.

Intercession also, happily, takes us out of ourselves and our self-preoccupation, and deepens our love both for others and for God. When you hold a friend and Jesus together in your thoughts, your appreciation and affection for both of them increases.

What words we use in our times of intercession are secondary. It may be simply a repeated aspiration: "Sacred Heart of Jesus, I place all my trust in you." Or that all-purpose prayer from the Desert Fathers: "Lord, as you know best, have mercy." Such prayers entrust your friend to Our Lord's care and leave it to him to do what is best for them.

Without any words you can allow your imagination to express your wishes – picturing your needy friend happy and at their best again, as you would want them to be. Or picturing Our Lord, or Our Lady, holding them in their arms and restoring them to health and peace and safety.

Tennyson's words are worth recalling at more length:

> Pray for my soul. More things are wrought by prayer
>
> Than this world dreams of. Wherefore, let thy voice
>
> Rise like a fountain for me night and day.
>
> For what are men better than sheep or goats...
>
> If, knowing God, they lift not hands of prayer
>
> Both for themselves and those who call them friend? ■

Prayer

Lord Jesus Christ, ascended into heaven,

You intercede for us night and day before the Father.

Teach me to become, in my turn, an intercessor for others.

Teach me to forget myself and allow my heart to go out to those in need.

Teach me to develop the habit of praying every day for those I love, for those I have hurt or wronged, for those who need my prayers.

For the rest of this visit, I will let their faces, one by one, linger gently in my mind

and ask you to bless them with the graces they need most at this time.

Every time I come to Mass, every time I come to pray, I bring them with me.

Whatever love you pour out on me, whatever grace you give to me, let it flow into them as well – to help them in their troubles, to heal them, to strengthen them, to bring them to deep, deep peace.

Lord, as you know best, have mercy!

Visit
19

Cosmos

I n the Eucharist we are at the heart of the universe. *Cosmos*, the ancient Greeks called it, a word meaning 'orderly arrangement,' the opposite of chaos. Like people of all cultures, they had observed, and carefully followed, the patterns and regularities of the heavenly bodies.

This regularity and orderliness of the cosmos is the necessary working assumption of all science to this day; without it science would be impossible. It is implied in the account of creation in the first chapter of Genesis, which depicts God making cosmos out of chaos.

Although a child can confidently tell us that God made the world out of nothing, the idea of creation-out-of-nothing is a hugely subtle, sophisticated philosophical and theological notion, not easy to grasp with the mind. A lovely imaginative way of thinking about it was offered in recent years: God sustains the universe as a singer sustains a song. This image implies the Spirit, or Breath, of the Singer, and the Word, or Sound, that he utters. It also conveys the delight of God in creation. 'God saw that it was good,' Genesis tells us many times. 'Good' can also be translated as 'beautiful.'

The first Christians, their minds illuminated by the bright light of the Resurrection, re-read the Old Testament – the only scripture they had for many years – and found Christ in its every nook and cranny, foreshadowed and foretold in prophets, psalms and histories.

Led by the Holy Spirit, they realised also the ever-widening implications of what God had accomplished in Christ. The event of Cross-Resurrection-Pentecost was not merely a matter of personal salvation of souls, but the beginning of a new creation, or re-creation, of the entire cosmos.

The extraordinary first chapter of Ephesians spells out the thrilling realisation by St Paul that God's plan for 'the fullness of time' was 'to unite all things in Christ, things in heaven and things on earth.'

'All things were created through him and for him,' says Paul in Colossians. 'He is before all things, and in him all things hold together.'

Recent scientific discoveries have excitingly reinforced our awareness of the unity and inter-relatedness of everything in the cosmos. We are made of stardust. The stuff of our world, including our bodies, was once the dust and debris of long-since exploded stars. And if Pascal, philosopher and scientist in the 17th century, knew as much as we do of the mind-blowing vastness of the cosmos, he would have trembled all the more before 'the infinite silence of the interstellar spaces.'

So, with Pascal, we can tremble in awe at the glory of creation. And with Hopkins we can kiss our hands to the stars, newly aware of 'the Cosmic Christ.' ∎

Prayer

Lord Jesus, King of Creation, I adore you.

The Bread of the Eucharist, here before me,

'fruit of the earth and work of human hands,'

is the very stuff of the universe itself,

made of the atoms and particles that once made up the stars.

In transforming bread into yourself you make all matter holy;

you reaffirm and deepen the goodness and beauty of

creation.

Enlarge my sense of the greatness of things,

my awareness of being caught up with you in the great drama

of the world's re-making and redemption.

Teach me to rejoice as the ingenuity of scientists

unveils more and more of the complexity and surprisingness

of the cosmos.

May I, too, tremble with awe before the silence of the spaces

between the stars.

May I tremble with awe at the thought that the One through

whom and for whom all that exists was made

is here with me, humbly hidden, but wholly given, in the

Bread of Life.

Visit
20   Good companions

The principal reason for reading the classics of literature, G.K. Chesterton said, is 'to keep us from being merely modern.'

Any age, ours included, allows only a limited realisation of the human potential for thinking, knowing and living. Other ages realised different aspects of the human repertoire, so knowing about them and entering into their experience by means of books and stories broadens our awareness of the richness of being human, and humbles our tendency to think we are the first to get things really right.

Our Church tradition, with its long memory, its storehouse of knowledge and practices, its books of wisdom and biography, its steady reverence for the past, is an invaluable culture in which our full humanity can expand. The very word 'catholic,' which describes us, means 'in tune with the whole,' with all of reality in its depth and height, and in its spread across time and space.

This is why remembering is such a vital part of Church life. Amnesia deprives us of our identity, renders us unfit for living in the present.

And that is why we have saints.

Saints are men, women and children who have lived life fully and intensely. They remind us of our own capacity for largeness of life. They awaken generous intentions and ambitions in our souls. They are our companions on our journey through life, in that precious reality of our faith we call 'the Communion of Saints.'

The word 'companion' is apt, the *pan* in the middle being the Latin word for bread. Com-pan-ions are those who share bread with us in friendship.

Our saints have, like us, been nourished by the Bread of the Eucharist. They also break the Bread of God's Word for us, by their living of it and their writing about it.

When Donald Nichol, an inspiring English writer and lecturer on the faith, was dying of cancer, he found he could no longer read or even think. So he prayed by simply gazing at the images on the walls of his room: the crucifix, Our Lady, and the saints and heroes who had captured his affections as he studied and taught history.

His companions in life, they were still his companions as he set out on his final journey, bringing him courage and reassurance.

Stroll around your church. Reacquaint yourself with the companions you find in statue, picture and window. Gaze, and let their memory linger gently in your mind. ▪

Prayer

My Lord Jesus Christ,

beginning with the apostles, how many companions you have drawn to yourself down the ages –

men, women and children from every time and country.

They fell under your spell. You awakened their souls. They blossomed.

Many were shining lights to the world.

Most were humble, heroic souls whose beauty was known only to you and to the few among whom they spent their lives.

I bless you, Lord, and thank you for these lovely people.

They are my companions, too.

They shared and were nourished by the same Bread of Life I now adore.

They heard and responded to your Word.

Make me more aware of them – these clouds of witnesses, as scripture calls them, who are especially close to us in the celebration of the Eucharist.

Awaken my soul as you awakened theirs.

Enchant me as you enchanted them.

Lord Jesus, I love you, and want to love you more and more.

Visit
21

Enchantment

T he French priest-philosopher, Stanislaus Breton, said that what first drew him to philosophy was reading 'books that sang to me.' 'Enchanted' was the word he used, making us aware of the 'chant,' the singing, that is at its heart. We are enchanted when someone or something sings to us, making our hearts sing in response.

The great enchantment for Christians, most notable in the saints, is the person of our Lord Jesus Christ. Again and again in the Gospels we read of the delighted astonishment he awoke in people; he enchanted them.

In the case of St Alphonsus, this enchantment with Jesus led literally to singing. He was an accomplished musician and wrote songs and hymns that are still sung in his native Italy after nearly three hundred years. A brilliant lawyer and theologian, he also had the ability and the passion to bring the best theology within the grasp of ordinary people through his popular writings on the spiritual life.

In 1745 – his life spanned most of the 18th century – he produced a little book of *Visits to the Blessed Sacrament* that has had enormous influence in the spiritual formation of Catholics ever since. It has never been out of print.

At first glance, it might seem to us to be somewhat old-fashioned, even sentimental, in its piety. But, of course, it reflects the time and culture out of which it came, as do the writings of, say, Dickens or Shakespeare. They can all still delight us and expand our knowledge of human life.

The affectionate feeling in Alphonsus is not sentimental: it flows from deep experience of the love of God, underpinned by extensive knowledge of scripture and theology.

Indeed, the *Visits* are largely a tapestry of quotations from scripture and from the saints, woven into a passionate unity by Alphonsus. Reading them dilates our minds and sets free our too-reined-in religious feelings. They convey to us that it is good to delight in the enchantment of Our Lord, to allow ourselves to be captivated by him, and to let our whole being sing in response. ■

Prayer

Lord, I thank you for St Alphonsus, and for all the saints whose words and stories he presents to us.

"Paradise for God," he says, "is the human heart."

What a startling, daring statement!

But it is what you have said to us throughout scripture:

"My delight is to be with the children of men."

"You shall no longer be called Foresaken, but my Delight."

No wonder Alphonsus spoke of your wonderfully insane love for us.

His prayer for the beginning of every visit I now make my own:

My Lord Jesus Christ, out of love for humankind, you remain night and day in this sacrament, awaiting, calling and welcoming all who come to visit you. I believe you are present here... I adore you from the depths of my being, and I thank you for all the graces you have bestowd on me, especially for giving me yourself in the Eucharist, for giving me your Mother Mary as my advocate, and for calling me to visit you in this church. My Jesus, I love you with my whole heart. I grieve for having so many times offended your infinite goodness. I now consecrate myself to you without reserve. All I ask and desire is your holy love, that I be faithful to the end, and always live according to your will, my Lord and my God.

Visit
22
Intimations

I ntimations of God come to us in a million ways – in a piece of fine music, in an eloquent picture or a sky full of stars, in a whiff of incense or fresh bread, in the touch of the wind or a kind hand on the face, in a sentence from a book or a sermon, in the taste of wine on the palate. Life is dense with such intimations – atheists have to guard their atheism very carefully! – and over time they converge and coalesce and make our Yes of faith possible, indeed, we might almost say, inevitable. 'Only a fool,' Psalm 14 begins bluntly, 'could say in his heart there is no God.'

Our more inward experiences also lead us to God.

A serious decision of conscience, for example, has a profound religious dimension and can make us sharply aware of standing before a transcendant Court of Judgement.

Becoming aware, usually over time, of a more-than-random pattern in the events of our life can also compel us to recognise a Providence at work and a graciousness taking care of us.

Or we may know God as the object of our spiritual yearning. Once our desires have moved beyond material things and reach out in a pure search for something more, we have really found God, for it is God who has made us to be seekers and uses our restless incompleteness to draw us to himself.

In a remarkable poem, which he calls *Missing God*, Dennis O'Driscoll sketches a series of ordinary 'secular' experiences that carry within them an ache for the absent God. The aches he describes – at a civil wedding or non-religious funeral, hearing plainchant on the radio, standing before a painting of the crucifixion in an art gallery – are the tug of God's love, still seeking us in the secular desert.

Strange though it may seem, even the painful experience of God's absence implies the realness of God, as thirst indicates the reality of water, or loneliness the reality of an absent person.

Perhaps the most precious and convincing way we become aware of God is in the simple knowledge that God is there, present, that God simply and gloriously *IS*. When we say Yes to this knowledge, perhaps hesitantly at first, and then with increasing wholeheartedness, faith flowers fully in us. Our whole being cries Amen.

"For me," wrote the French philosopher Rene le Senne, "the principal proof of the existence of God is the joy I experience any time I think that God is." ■

Prayer

Lord Jesus Christ, you approach, touch and awaken me
through all my senses, through my mind,
my imagination, my feelings, my entire being.
And my entire being goes out to you in faith, hope and love.
I pray with the psalm, 'O God, *you* are my God, for *you* I long.
For *you* my soul is thirsting.
My body pines for you, like a dry, weary land without water.
On my bed I remember you; on you I muse through the night.
My soul clings to you; your right hand holds me fast.'
Jesus, you have awakened my soul.
Through the years, in all the happenings of my life,
you have been seeking me, guiding me, taking care of me.
Most of the time I didn't realise you were there,
but you were patient and understanding, waiting for me.
Now, at last, I come to thank you, to 'watch with you a while,'
to be at peace in your company,
and let your love and forgiveness flow into me.
You are my Lord and my God.

I n our everyday speech words tend to be simple and
functional, but in formal situations we instinctively use words
more carefully, giving them a heightened, more intense
quality – in a parliamentary address, say, or a funeral oration.

Words become most heightened and most intense in poetry
and in religious ceremonies. Then they draw us out of the
ordinary and break open our minds and hearts to deeper and
richer realities. They lift us above the familiar, expanding our
capacity for understanding and response.

Sometimes they take on an awesome power, as in great poetry,
and even more as in the Mass: "This is my Body." Both scripture
and liturgy reach for poetic utterance in their effort to disclose in
some measure the mysteries of God, to express the inexpressible.
Our effort then must be to 'inhabit the words,' as it were, to enter
into them and let them carry us into the realities they embody.

In an otherwise satirical poem, TS Eliot has a few moving lines
about a painting of the Baptism of Jesus which depicts Our
Lord standing in the shallows of the Jordan.

Eliot writes: But through the water pale and thin
            Still shine the unoffending feet...

'Shine,' of course, suggests the radiance of the divine, but the
wondrously right word here is 'unoffending.' It is lovely in its
sound and resonant with the meaning of Our Lord's whole life.
It renders the original, earthy sense of the word 'innocent,'

which is from two Latin words meaning 'not wounding', 'not injuring', 'not offending.'

The Lamb of God! The power and far-reachingness of one word.

"Lamb of God... grant us peace," we pray at Mass. The word 'peace' is thin in sound and thin in meaning compared to the Hebrew word Jesus would have used when he said, "My peace I give you." *Shalom* is still used by Jewish people in their everyday greeting of one another. It does mean peace, of course, but much more – harmony, health and wholeness, total well-being. It connotes nearly all that we mean by salvation. "He is our peace," our *shalom*, St Paul says of Christ. The very sound *shalom* has a fullness and music that rolls satisfyingly on the tongue.

Amen is another Hebrew word we tend to miss the fullness of – again, two syllables that were frequently on the lips of Jesus. It means "Yes, with all my heart," or "Yes, that is the truth," or "Oh, may it be true!"

('So be it' is a curt and thin translation, quite lacking in the strength and feeling of the original.)

The Jesuit theologian, Fr Michael Paul Gallagher, suggests as the shortest definition of faith, 'A YES to a YES.' God says yes to us in love, and we say yes to God in response. This is the quality of yes that Amen conveys. Every time we say it, it could be a wholehearted act of faith, a word wholly inhabited by us. Or it might be a cry from the heart for more faith – "Oh, may it be so!" ■

Prayer

My Lord Jesus Christ, I say Amen to you.

I believe. Help my unbelief. Amen, Amen!

I say Amen to your presence with me in the Eucharist.

It is so great a gift, how can I not say Amen with all my heart.

Isaiah speaks of 'the God of Amen,' the God of Truth, the God of Yes.

Revelation calls you 'The Amen, the faithful and true witness, the source of God's creation.'

You are God's Yes to creation – 'God saw that it was good.'

And you are God's even more resounding Yes to Redemption, the New Creation.

Thank you, dear Lord. Amen, Amen, Amen!

Visit
24

Word of God

When we speak of God we can only do so by using comparisons and parallels from human experience - metaphors and analogies, in more technical terms. "The Lord is my shepherd, my rock, my fortress" – these are obvious metaphors. But Father, Son and Holy Spirit are also analogous terms for the mystery that is always beyond human speech.

Scripture uses the word 'Holy' to indicate the complete difference of God from everything else. Its root meaning is 'separate' or 'different' or 'completely other.' It's what Isaiah heard the angels singing in his vision of the heavenly court: Holy, Holy, Holy! – Different, different, different! We join in that ecstatic singing at Mass, acclaiming God as unlike anything or anyone else, utterly beyond us.

"Heaven and earth are full of your glory," we go on to sing. 'Glory' is the radiance in creation of God's 'otherness' or 'beyond-all-ness.' Holy and Glory are words to be uttered with the greatest reverence and awe.

The glory of God filling heaven and earth are conveyed by another analogy in the first chapter of Genesis. God is presented there as 'speaking' creation into existence. Each of the six days begins, 'God said', 'God spoke.' 'God spoke *light* and there was light.'

When we speak we express or utter something that was previously inside us. 'Express' (Latin again) means 'push out,' and 'utter' is a variation of 'outer' – to bring *out* what was within.

To imagine God speaking, then, is to think of God 'outering' or 'ex-pressing' something that was within him. Imperfect though it is, this image gives us some purchase on the mystery of creation and the relation of created things to the transcendant mystery of God. Everything that exists is a word of God, expressing something of God's mind and heart, radiant with something of God's truth, goodness and beauty, bubbling over in delight from the 'boiling ocean of love,' as Eckhart puts it, that is the vivacious, effervescent, Holy Trinity.

Contemplated in this light, nothing in the world will ever be the same again. We will see things as Jesus saw them, words of love spoken anew every morning. ■

Prayer

Lord Jesus, for you this world and everything in it was the outpouring of your Father's love, pure gift, to be delighted in and to give thanks for.

Teach me to see things as you did, with wide, wondering eyes, like a child.

Lead me into an attitude of reverence and gratitude for all that is, especially for every human being, all of us, like you, the image of our Father.

But you are the last word, the most perfect expression of the Father's mind and heart.

"When you have seen me," you said to Phillip, "you have seen the Father."

You are "the image of the invisible God," as St Paul says.

Lord, I have some sense of the Father's creative word from the power of your words in the Eucharist: This is my Body.

May I learn to give more weight and intent to the words I utter at Mass – words like Holy, and Glory and Amen.

And may the words of scripture come more alive for me and awaken my soul to more generous and wholehearted prayer.

Lamb of God, have mercy on me and grant me peace.

Say but the word and my soul shall be healed.

Visit
25

Paradise

The word 'paradise' comes from an ancient Persian or Iranian word meaning 'garden' – the elaborately designed garden of a king or emperor, rich with flowers, trees and fruit, watered by streams, warrened with paths, sweet with birdsong and the sounds of fountains and leaves. It's easy to see how it came to be an image of heaven and total happiness.

The Bible depicts all human history as taking place between two gardens: the garden of Eden and the garden promised by Jesus to the dying thief on Calvary – "This day you will be with me in paradise." Between the two occurs the drama of human muddle and mayhem.

All of us tend to have imaginations of both, of a paradise lost and a paradise to come, the one stirring us to nostalgia and tears, the other to longing and hope. Both express deep truths of our faith.

It is told that Russia began to be converted to Christianity in the 10th century when ambassadors of Prince Vladimir of Kiev attended Mass in the church of Santa Sophia in Constantinople (now Istanbul). They reported to their prince that it was so beautiful they didn't know whether they were in heaven or still on the earth. The prince decided that this was the religion for his people. Russia was converted by the beauty of the liturgy.

Even a quiet, simple Mass has an enchanting beauty for those who get lost in it. And the dullest of us usually have a peace in ourselves at the end of Mass that was not there at the beginning. As well as being a memorial of things past, Mass is also a promise and foretaste of paradise. We are with Jesus and, in its essence, heaven is where Jesus is. And he will have kept the promise we remind him of just before communion: "I leave you peace. My peace I give you."

In the Eucharist the borders between heaven and earth dissolve. We join the angels and the saints in their song of joy: 'Holy, Holy, Holy…Heaven and Earth are full of your glory.' 'Through Him, with Him, in Him' we sense the radiant truth and beauty of the Trinity, Father, Son and Holy Spirit.

What will heaven be like? We have inklings, imaginings, longings and hope, but it is really beyond us.

Fr Sean O'Riordan, a beloved Redemptorist theologian and spiritual adviser, was asked on his deathbed how he felt about dying. He managed a small smile and said, "I'm looking forward to the surprises."

Surprise there will be, out of this world. But as the final and everlasting enchantment begins, might there be some faint sense of "Have I been here before?"

Ah, yes… those Eucharists! ∎

Prayer

Lord Jesus Christ, all my hope of paradise is in you.

"I go to prepare a place for you," you tell us, "so that where I am you will be too."

Wherever you are is heaven. So heaven is already here, hidden but real, as you are in the Blessed Sacrament.

I thank you for the peace that comes over me when I enter your house.

I thank you for all the churches, great and small, built all over the world, each a 'heaven's reflex,' a haven of peace, where poor wandering, sometimes lost,

souls like myself can come, to have our burdens lightened, our fears allayed, our hearts lifted,

our hope renewed – that there *is* a paradise,

a garden of delight, where all tears will be wiped away,

all hurts healed, all brokenness mended,

and our astonished souls will see you, face to face.

Visit
26   Room for all

A hundred or so years ago, many people involved in the national and social movements of the time had difficulties with disapprovals and condemnations from Church authorities. Referring to this later, the author James Plunkett wrote: 'Yet for mature men of my childhood, even those who had suffered from its intolerance, the Church guarded a Truth which was better than all its wrongheadedness.'

That truth, of course, is Jesus and all he stands for. The Church keeps his memory alive, not just for Catholics, but for the whole world. Without the Church the memory of Jesus would have been lost long since. The Church told his story from the very beginning, memorised it, passed it on, eventually wrote it down in the Gospels, and has continued to transmit and interpret it to every generation.

Unpromisingly small when Jesus first gathered it and said, "Do this in memory of me," the Church began to celebrate the Eucharist which nourishes us to this day. Without the Church, this moment of Eucharistic grace in your life would not be happening. There would be no Easter, no Christmas, no sacraments.

The word 'church' comes from the Greek word for 'belonging to the Lord.' We are those who belong to the Lord, and the church building is the house of God.

Another Greek, and Latin, word for Church is *ecclesia*. It means 'those who are called together.' St John's Gospel says that Jesus died 'to gather together all the scattered children of God.' That has been happening and will go on happening till the end of time. Jesus promised to be with his Church till then and has given the Holy Spirit to be the soul of the Church, the giver of its life.

When a man, sophisticated and knowledgeable in the ways of the world, recently became a Catholic, he was asked, "What drew you to the Church?" "I saw," he replied, "that there was room and welcome in the Church for sinners like me." A good reason for becoming a Catholic, and a good reason for staying one.

The name Jesus means 'God saves.' It has an underlying meaning of 'God makes room.' A lovely thought to expand our notions of salvation and creation, to throw light on God's accommodation of our freedom, and to think of along with Our Lord's words: "In my Father's house there are many rooms."

Catholic means 'all-embracing', 'in tune with the whole of reality.' A wise and saintly French Jesuit, Fr Jules Monchanin, urges that we "dilate the Church with our prayers." Now there's a mission! ∎

Prayer

Lord Jesus, my Lord and my God,

in contrast to the expansiveness of your mind and vision,

and to the all-embracingness of your Church,

how pinched and ungenerous are my mind and heart.

I am so lacking in magnanimity, largeness of soul.

"Let this mind – and imagination – be in you," says St Paul,

"that was in Christ Jesus."

But I continue to be self-preoccupied and petty in my judgements.

"Be merciful," you tell me, "as your heavenly Father is merciful."

Teach me to dilate my own heart, to make room there for your concerns and those of your Church.

Teach me to be understanding and cheerfully patient with my not-yet-perfect fellow Catholics. Teach me to be thankful and happy to belong to your Church, the ark you have built for us to carry us safely over the stormy sea of life.

Visit
27 A woman of few words

There was a moment in history when the fate of the cosmos was in a woman's hands. Future generations held their breath – in a certain sense even God held his breath! – in the split second of waiting for Mary's Yes to the angel's message. "Look at me," came her wholehearted response, "Here I am... Let it be done to me according to your word." In that moment 'the Word was made flesh' in a young woman's womb, a new future opened up for humanity, the age-old dreams and yearnings of the world began to be fulfilled.

It took God many generations of preparing, educating and refining the spirit of his people before they gave birth to this girl. She was the culmination of the long line of outstanding women who had played decisive roles at crucial moments in Israel's history – Eve, Hannah, Deborah, Judith, Esther. The song of thanksgiving, *Magnificat*, that Mary sang on her visit to Elizabeth is a tissue of Old Testament thoughts and phrases, echoing particularly the thanksgiving of Hannah for the birth of her son, Samuel. In Mary all that was good and pure and godly in her people reached its finest flowering.

Apart from the Magnificat, only a few words of hers are recorded in the Gospels. "How can this be?" she asks the angel at the Annunciation, not in doubt or protest, but in 'faith seeking understanding,' as St Anselm defined theology centuries later. Then came her "Here I am," that deep response of Israel to God, learnt, no doubt, from her parents, Joachim and Anne.

On finding the boy Jesus in the Temple she asks, again seeking to understand: "Why have you done this to us?" This son of hers was always stretching her faith, but she responded every time, 'pondering these things in her heart.'

Her only other recorded words occur at the marriage in Cana, when, with the simple statement, "They have no wine," she occasions an epiphany, a shining out of the glory of her Son, in the miracle of the water-into-wine. "Do whatever he tells you," she says, giving us an ideal to live by till the end of time.

To each of his *Visits to the Blessed Sacrament*, St Alphonsus added a Visit to Mary.

His love for her was deep and tender, his confidence in her intercession unbounded. He knew that, like the shepherds at Christmas, we find Jesus with his Mother.

After our visit to Jesus in the Eucharist, we do well to follow Alphonsus in paying our respects to Our Lady – to invoke her intercession, to honour her with Hail Marys, the Memorare, the Hail Holy Queen, to thank her for saying Yes on our behalf all those years ago, for giving us 'the blessed fruit of her womb, Jesus.' ∎

Prayer

Lord Jesus Christ, Son of God, Son of Mary,

your Mother gave you to us,

and, on the cross, you gave us to her, committing us to her motherly care.

What profound affection must have flowed between your Mother and you!

And yet, even before Calvary, her tears flowed, too,

as she followed the alarming course of your life, its dangers and mysteries.

Her first Yes was costly; the sword of suffering often pierced her soul, as Simeon had foretold. Yet she was faithful to the end.

The image of her final grief, holding your lifeless body in her arms at the foot of the cross, haunts the human imagination ever since, strangely and beautifully reassuring to all whose hearts are breaking.

Lord Jesus, I honour your Mother.

She it was who gave us the Body and Blood I now adore here in the Eucharist.

When I come to her, I come to you.

When I come to you, I come to her.

Praised be Jesus and Mary!

Visit
28

Meditation

St Alphonsus in the 18th century quotes St Bernard in the 12th saying that silence and the absence of tumult almost force the soul to think of heavenly things. In the 7th century St John Climacus says that "intelligent silence is the mother of prayer." (So much is implied in that word 'intelligent.') Saint after saint down the ages could be quoted to the same effect.

But in our Catholic tradition they all take for granted that the one who enters into silence and stillness takes with them a mind and imagination already furnished with the stories and teachings of the faith, and that these stories and teachings continue to underlie the silence, keeping us steady and on 'the Way' in an otherwise pathless void. Even the most advanced contemplatives, like St Teresa and St John of the Cross, never let go of their grip on the down-to-earth particulars of the faith, especially and above all on the person of Jesus.

In this final reflection, with a view to continuing and deepening our prayer, let us recall the simple method St John of the Cross used to teach his Carmelite novices as a guiding structure for their hour of meditation, to focus and discipline their minds and imaginations. The Gospels – heard, read or remembered – are the starting point.

1 The first thing is to call to mind the stories – the mysteries John calls them – of Jesus, by imagining them in a general, impressionistic way. Allow yourself to enter the scene, to be present to Jesus as he prays in a lonely place, or cures a blind person, or calms the stormy sea.

2 Then ponder in your mind the epiphany you have called up, allowing your mind and imagination to draw you further into its depths and implications.

3 Then relax into simple attentiveness to God, in loving stillness, desiring God, adoring God, asking God – going with whatever prayer has been awakened in you.

The standard starting point for such meditative prayer is a reading of the Gospels. But they, in turn, point to the whole Bible as filling out the central mystery of Jesus. He himself points us in that direction, especially in his 'opening of the scriptures' to the disciples after the Resurrection.

"Take and read," St Augustine heard a child's voice telling him one day in the garden. He took up the scriptures and began to read, and the world began to change, illuminated by the light of Christ.

As soon as we begin to read, with quiet attentiveness and desire, prayer begins in us, and our world, too, will begin to change. ∎

Prayer

Lord Jesus Christ, Light of the world,

open the scriptures for me as you did for your disciples after your Resurrection.

Help me to read every story in the Gospels as an epiphany, a shining out of your mystery, awakening my soul and lighting up my path through life.

Teach me to pray as you taught the disciples

- the Our Father, which sums up your whole vision and mission
- the psalms, which you prayed and which I can pray along with you, thus entering your mind and heart.

Teach me the discipline of setting aside a regular time and place for meditation.

Stir up the desire in my soul to be with you, to delight in knowing and loving you,

to discover the joy of following your Way.

Your Way, O Lord, is my delight.

Appendix

Tantum Ergo
Richard Tobin, C.Ss.R.

Eyes see bread, but faith sees Jesus
In this mystery of grace.
God is with us, as he promised,
Here and through all time and space.
Come, believer, and adore him;
Lift your voice in songs of praise.

Praise the Father, life unending;
Praise the Son, his heart's delight;
Praise the Spirit, love out-flowing;
Praise them to the heavens' height.
Heaven's here, where God is with us,
Love and truth and beauty bright.
Amen.

Adoro Te
Richard Tobin, C.Ss.R.

Jesus, see us kneeling
Here before you,
Gathered in one body
To adore you.
What the whole world hungers for
Given here we find –
God's own self in form of bread,
Food for humankind.

Cross and Passion we recall
And your death for us.